THE BLACK PEARL:

NAKED AND NOT ASHAMED

Dr. Julia Mims Robinson

Author's Tranquility Press
ATLANTA, GEORGIA

Dr. Julia Mims Robinson /Author's Tranquility Press
3800 CAMP CREEK PKWY SW BLDG 1400-116 #1255
Atlanta, GA 30331
www.authorstranquilitypress.com
Ordering Information:

Quantity sales. Special discounts are available on quantity purchases by
corporations, associations, and others. For details, contact the "Special
Sales Department" at the address above.

THE BLACK PEARL / Dr. Julia Mims Robinson
Hardback: 978-1-959930-62-4
Paperback: 978-1-959930-63-1
eBook: 978-1-959930-64-8

CONTENTS

Prayer

O, Lord, we seek you.

Hear our request as we present
our voices of praise and thanksgiving.
Hear our groans and plead or causes.
Lord, we need your Divine Intervention.
Merciful, Gracious Father,
hear our cry.

Bless the works of your servant and all the participants. Help
us to forever uplift your son Jesus.

In the beauty of Holiness
The ones that read these writings,
bless and keep them safe.
Lord, we all live in troubled times.
Oh, how we need your guidance.

Bless us, we pray.
In Jesus' name,

AMEN.

Dedication

I pray will be an inspiration to all who invest energy in reading this book. To invest time and effort will give you a deeper insight in the worth of the Black Pearl. I hope you will laugh with me and also shed a tear at some of life circumstances encountered in my life challenge. Inspire to be the best you that breathe the breath of life and to devote a greater emphasis in prayer. It's my dream that this book will expire you to invest quality time in getting to know yourself. Listening to the voice of God in the quietness of your day while you're getting reacquainted with who you think you are rather than who you are. God wants to introduce you a deeper realm of understanding rather that common emotions exist in daily living.

Dr. Julia Mims Robinson

My Prayer

I thank you, Lord, for this moment in time.
Each breath you allow me to take,
Each second to breathe.

Thank you for giving me a generous portion of your goodness
and mercy,
another portion of strength for today's tasks,
and for encouraging me and providing strength for every task
encountered.

Thank you for watching over my every move and keeping me
out of harm's way.
Thank you for sending your Holy Spirit to guide me each
day.

Thank you for keeping me focused on my journey ahead.

In Jesus' name,

AMEN.

Heart Balcony

Feeling high and lifted up.
Energetically narrow the visual field.
Heart repeals issues that causes
pain to surface or anger to peep.

Heart enhances issues that produces peace.
Pleasure and goodness lean hard
on the balcony of forgiveness and
forgetting events of discord.

Heart's Balcony will have several climbers.
Chance will climb, just don't let chance overstep
common sense.

Step softly on my Balcony,
the Boardwalk might not be for you.

The Balcony of My Heart is reserved,
not for casual travelers,
nor for adventure seekers,
For that special traveler seeking
when pressure start rising.
It will come and person
that is occasional climber
will not be able to handle the pressure.

They will be just another traveler
that the wind blew away.
Storms of my life challenges surface,
wind began to blow and
storms of life challenges come.

It will send them in uncharted directions. They will lose
around and fade away.

The Balcony of My Heart is
not for the occasional chancer,
they will blow as wind
and fade as evening sun.

The Balcony of My Heart is
not for casual climbers,
nor for slick and crafty,
but for pure in heart.
My Heart Balcony must be cherished.

Black Pearl

Pressure deep in the facet of nature, concentration under diverse distress, naked and not ashamed as it goes undetected for season in the realm of unrealistic reality. Issues lie dominate in the soul until media presents itself.

Stress induced for extended period will cause initial grain of sand to become embedded in network of emotions. Blossom into network of emotions. Blossom into dimension of emotions that inhibits the normal response to function at the rate to ward off variant invaders.

History of misunderstanding, verbal abuse, physical abuse is seen as ultimate trigger that led that grain of sand multiplying to a degree that mature as the coated grain of sand in medium get longer and longer. With time and various circumstance, the grain of sand changes with pressure. Strength imitates circumstances as confronted with pressure. Life is forever changing as it evolve the reader looks back as it confronts each issue.

Life shifts to the realm as it become unbearable. Change become evident that the coating in the oyster harden, producing stone from grit. As life events bring about changing in humanity that give rise to strength to keep marching forward, despite hardship and disappointments.

In life, you are faced with challenges almost beyond comprehension, yet you survive with grave struggles. Your faith in Jesus you become destined to change, that is evident to the outer layer of pressure becomes harder, as it changes texture, to meet with the forces of stress presented. The changing texture noted in the pearl denotes life alteration in physical as the pearl changes its coat to equal pressure, excited in the challenges under pressure. The oyster secretion hardens, symbolic of life with layer shift to develop new strategies of coping.

In life, we are faced with issues beyond our finite comprehension. The grit within us keeps the irritation so uncomfortable that giving up is not an option. The true test come when you pray, and things instead get worse instead of relief.

At this point, it's in Faith challenge, Faith walks, still no relief. Your destiny is slowly slipping away, chances of recovery are slim. Still, you seek an alternative to survive anyway, anyhow. I must survive.

At this phase, the pressure of the grit within the oyster is overbearing. The secretion that is covering the grain of sand that at this point has changed from a pearly white to a darker shade of gray and you're at that point ready to throw in the towel. Yet you say, "Not yet!"

USE LESS NESS

It's useless to labor all day
for self-worth without the worth
being kept by the Creator–
which giveth worth to the substance
of the soul.

Labor is taxing and troubling,
equal the production of worth,
as weariness to the soul.

In the depths of weariness
is the making of greatness,
if not allowed to drain the soul.

Mind, will, and emotion
propel the essence of total being
that exist in the presence of Use Less Ness.

Shipwreck

Life challenge overbearing
Turbulence swirling
Wind blowing
Bellow ragging
Shipwrecked on Sea of Life Lost my life raft
I'm sinking
Help me, Jesus
Sinking
Cannot survive
Shark near, tongue wagging

Help!
Help!
Help!

Foe against me
trying to take me under.

Hurt is all around me.
I don't want failure, can't swim.
What am I to do?

Thunder roaring
Fearful of sinking, can't swim. Is there no hope for me?

I'm sinking without you, Lord.

Certainly crash
Is there any hope for me?

Shipwreck! Shipwreck!
On Sea of Life.

Escape

Pain is imminent.
Overbearing
No relief, no analgesic

Sabbatical is emetic.
Mute button on

No response
Consciousness alerted.

Escape
Escape
Escape

Where to?
To the Cross!

So, do not fear, for I am with you.
Do not be dismayed, for I am your God.
-Isaiah 41:10

Shadows

Looking through the lens of my soul
Something blurred is following me
It's distorted when I turn

It turns
It's blurred, keep following me
It's not for me to discern
Just keep following me.

I stand still, the lens reveal a secret
It's standing still
Shadow, Shadow, Shadow

Looks like me
When I turn, it turns
I skip, it skips
What is it?

I'm stressed, unable to reason
I'm afraid
Will knowledge reveal the secret of the shadow?

What Is It?

Looking through my soul,
what is it?

Images are blurred
often times distorted.

It's not visible questions
in my mind, what is it?
Images blurred
Appears distorted
It's not for me to discern
at this moment I'm nervous
I must stand still
My lens is distorted
My soul is perplexed.
I must stand still
Focus on reality
I'm stressed.

Making decisions at this point is Faithless
Not reasoning, I'm afraid
Stand still, you're able to focus
It's just my shadow chasing me!

Yesterday's Pearl

The toils of life have brought me to this point in life-struggling to maintain my sanity, seeing no end to the stressors. The struggle is real. Reflecting to the years of my youth that was engulfed in with difficult challenges. My energy was invested into being compliant with chaos around the house. Lack and need never meet. Yes, food was provided, clothing, and loving parents. Instituted the Pearl that tag along until this present day.

To identify the culprit and to make an interaction with unresolved issues. Getting to know myself was as issue that encompass many layers that must be peeled off gently.

As the layer is gently lifted, scars appear with flashes of history being revealed. Teary-eyed appear with phases of life unfolding. Memory is fragile and must be handled with care.

In the years from 5 years old, history was being revealed in layers. As a child sitting at my mother's knees listening to her while she combs my hair (this was her ritual twice a day at 5:00 AM for school and after getting home and the evening. I remember her relating specifically that I was born premature, weighing at 2 pounds and six ounces. I was in total shock. I looked at her like "What happened"? She paused for a moment. She said she fell while seven months pregnant. She was in the house and the floorboard was loose, her leg went through the floor. As a result, she gave birth to me.

When the midwife came, she had been prepared for her baby to be stillborn, so she brought a shoebox for the casket and a dress for the baby's burial. To her surprise,

I cried, and to this day my mother combs my hair as we converse history.

There was a long silent pause. The silence was unnerving. I spoke up, saying, "What next"? I could have slapped myself in the mouth. When I looked at my mother's face, I saw tears running down her cheeks.
I didn't ask what's wrong. I knew she was remembering an era that was painful. Therefore, I sat quietly for a while. Later, she stooped down and kissed my cheeks. Smiling as she kissed me again and again.

As I grew older, my mother misplaced things or couldn't find something she needed at a certain time. Momma would call me, Julia Mae! Go get whatever item she couldn't find and tell me to go get it. In my confused state of being, it was foreign for her to ask something of me when I didn't know what she was asking me to get. She would describe it to me and say," go find it"! and off I would go looking. To this day, I don't know why I could find every item she misplaced. I once heard her say that I'm gifted.

I couldn't understand my gift, but I grew to accept it. As I grew older, my memory was sharper with events of early childhood. On one occasion, I related to my mother about an incident that frightened me. I was in my baby bed and a dark shadow was on my face. I was wet and crying. "Why are you looking at me so weird"? Momma said. I cried for days. That was a memory at 6 months.

At 2 years of age, I remember sitting on the ground. I had soiled my diaper by putting sand in it. The sand was white. Momma said it was true, there was a sandbox in the yard, and it was filled with white sand.

Moving on, can't linger too long on my early adventure as a child but I will relate on of my life-changing event that changed my expectation about Salvation and moving of the Holy Spirit.

I was baptized at age 8 and accepted Jesus Christ as my personal savior. Our church didn't have a baptismal pool. The church was gathered and marched down the road to a sister church for baptism.We sang as we march along the road. Oh, what a time that was. After getting back that afternoon, my next-door neighbor had been bedridden for over 6 months. I asked momma if I can go to Mrs. Ransom. She asked me what I want to go there for. I replied I want to pray for her. I had never been inside the Ransom residence although we were next-door neighbors for many years. Momma said "Yes, go ahead. Just don't upset her". I immediately picked up my Bible and hasten to see Mrs. Ransom upon entering. I asked her if I can pray for her. She smiled and said "Yes, Julia Mae." I put my hand on her forehead and said a prayer. Then I left and went back home.

Later that day, Mrs. Ransom came out of her house sitting on the porch. I give God glory and Honor for all He has done.

Different, yes, I was different. There was a burning within my heart to know more and to have a closer walk with Jesus. There were times when I would go to church 7 days a week or as long as the service lasted. I received the Holy Spirit and had Joy. I loved the praise service.

Throughout my journey, I've made Jesus my personal friend. I was not ashamed to talk about Jesus, anywhere and even to my golden years. I say, "Oh now I love Jesus. He's my best friend. My Savior".

Safe Am I

Storm cloud, Thunder roaring
Lightning flashing,
Fierce wind blowing,
I am not afraid
Safe am I

Jesus hide me safely
In his loving care
Misunderstanding, confusion
burst like billows
As I stand trusting His promises

Flash lighting, roar thunder
You're under the control
I ride with Master in his Life Raft.
Wind believe, waves calm
Safe am I

Jesus is on board.
My Life Raft is Jesus.

Yesterday is Today

It's strange that today is so familiar to yesterday. It seems as if it's déjà vu. Been here before.

I found myself putting my clothes on over my nighties. My left shoe on my right foot, right on my left. No one can tell me any different. I got my shoes on.

Someone said to me it's raining outside. My mind is fixed. I like playing in the rain. There I go out in the rain. I hear voices calling me to come back.

I don't know why children play in rain. After all, it's not raining hard. I hear someone say "Oh, Lord. She's lost her mind." I chuckle to myself as I ran in the yard. It's so much fun. I said, "Catch me if you can!", down the street, running as fast as I can.

I heard people screaming, "Don't get out on the street, you can get hurt!" Oh, how fast I ran, saying to myself, "Catch me if you can!"

I heard squeaking of brakes; people screaming, "Stop! Stop! All the more, I ran up the street in path of cars. In my mind, I say you better get out my way 'cause I've got the rights.

Oh, how foolish, this must have been to think I'm a match for a car. I must have been startled because the car stopped.

The driver jumped out. Oh, how angry he looked yelling! "You must be out of your mind! Get out of the street!" He yelled.

Here come the troops, who grabbed me by the arm, pulling me out of the street. I said to myself, why are they so angry? I'm only playing. I could hear angry voices. "Lock her up, lock her up!" I lifted my head up saying I'm playing, it's raining. I like being in the rain.

A kind old lady came up to me and said, "Sugar, what you just did, you could have gotten hurt. Thank God you're alright."

I did not know what "I knew I had to do something. The freshly filled pitcher of ice was at my right hand I felt my hand pushing the pitcher on the floor. The nurse that was accomplishing me tripped over her cart spilling ice on the floor. We left the unit the two of us took a sick day. Thinking about it. Now, I have mixed emotions. Naked and not ashamed.

Black Pearl

The weight of Enchantment promotes creativity
toward balancing the necessities of life.

Worth in midst of turbulent times gives
rise to the nesting in the oyster.

Pressure, pressure, pressure.

Equal the nesting bed of worth.
Problems in the atmosphere swoop in the midst of
darkness in troubled waters.

Give rise to the Master Gem: The Black Pearl.

Black Pearl

Black Pearl of a Woman Naked without Ashamed written from a REALIST VEIW. This is a true story of a woman's life. It was not until her wounds had healed, and she was able to write about abuse she experienced. Some women protect their image by pretense, ignoring their feeling of being rejected. The pain of rejection may give rise to negative behavior. Destroying the image, you portrayed leading to utter despair and often into depression. Pain sends a decoy to detract the mind masking your true self. My self-esteem spring up to rescue me but self-worthlessness overrode it, while it tampered with my ego strength.

It became a giant as the woman within me slowly slips into uncertainty. Masked with fake smiles as a decoy, giving time to recover in unfamiliar territory. Only to be devoured by another wolf in sheep clothing. She is grouped as an article of clothing to be groped and pawed upon as a piece of property owned, with no rights. This is a form of abuse hidden under the disguise you know I love you...

It's Me

Looking through the lens of self-righteous telescope, it's me naked and not ashamed. My lens magnifies the minute fraction of your telescope yet minimize the errors. Not realizing that one day truth will birth itself without being acknowledged.

Don' wait until your moment of truth reveals itself. With revelation of truth comes pain, if not death, with the underlining issues, causes life alteration that is impossible to repair.

Here I am, naked and not ashamed of the issues in life accomplished and how many times I failed to live up to life's expectations through eyes of critics.

Guilty as charged, standing before the world telescope of criticism. Writing history. Mine alone can make the changes necessary to wipe out the blighted image portrayed in the spectrum of my truth.

Life has its peaks–highs and lows, guilty or innocent–the moving hand continues to mark time with the drummer.

Take your eyes off the cascade of time in your rearview mirror. It's only history, cannot be erased and never undone. I must embrace the truth and turn the page over because time marches on.

Be careful not to rewrite the last page. Just amend the fractions and look at the beauty of yesterday's mistakes. Move on, quickly!

The critics will always pick and choose which tangent to lift to the sky, and many times downplay the Pearl worth acknowledging.

Remember the eyes of critics will remain open, therefore, don't close your eyes. Be careful, yesterday's mistakes need not be the author of your epithets.

The pen is still actively adding strength to the Pearl. Therefore, keep moving.

Rear View Mirror

Our old house' front porch was covered with vines for shade in the summertime. As a child, my mother would sit for hours, rocking back and forth. Sometimes she would sit there until dawn. Many times, that rocking would be heard squeaking until dawn–back and forth– who would ever believe the squeaking throughout the night. She would sing "Oh what a time, my Lord."

One afternoon, while she was sitting in her favorite spot rocking back and forth, I came out and sat on the floor in front of her while she rocked. She didn't pay any attention to me. I just sat quietly, listening to her humming "Oh what a time, my Lord."

This day was different from others. It seems as if she was staring into space. She didn't even acknowledge my presence, just kept staring into space. I watched her for a while before asking what she was thinking. For a brief moment she didn't answer, nor did she acknowledge my presence.

Her gaze was so intense that it was difficult for me to follow the intensity of her staring. She sat silent without saying a word. It seemed as if she was looking into my soul. I felt uneasy.

Suddenly her gaze broke. She noticed the uneasiness that was felt and gently took my hand. She said, "Don't be afraid". She touched my face while she was talking and gently stroked my cheeks.

Oh, how gentle her touch was. Her fingers felt as if trying to apologize. I didn't know what to make of her remarks. I just said OK and positioned myself on the floor in front of her.

In my hand, I had her favorite comb that she used regularly to do my hair. I just wanted to be near her.

I gave her the comb while she began taking my braid apart to comb my hair. She was usually slow but this time she was unusually slower. I asked mom what she was thinking, she laughed. There was a silence. Her voice was trembling. I looked up and there were tears on her face. She began singing as she combed my hair. It seemed like hours sitting there in silence, just combing and fluffing my hair. Then she stopped. I started to get up. I touched my hair and said, "Mom, you haven't finished. You just took my hair loose".

I turned around and saw big tears running down her cheeks, shocked, as I stared at my champion. I didn't know what to say. I thought maybe she lost something, or I might have misplaced something or broken something which would account for her unusual behavior (as a child I was very inquisitive, I would go into things just to investigate them), which would account for her unusual silence.

This was different and overwhelming, as I looked at her again. Momma was crying. I began to cry because my champion was feeling pain. I didn't know why. I became frightened not knowing what to say or what to do.

Momma was crying and I also began to cry. I was staring at her face and there were uncontrollable tears streaming down her cheeks. Her voice was trembling.

"Momma, what's wrong"? I was curious, I didn't know what to say or how to respond.

Mom used snuff (Tube Rose), she put a scoop in her mouth. I watched as she settled the snuff in her lip. Finally, she said, "Sit here, let me tell you something". I was a busy little girl, often getting into her belongings, so I thought I may have broken something. I'm nervous now and shaking. I thought I'm gonna get it.

Her tears had something to do with me. I immediately began to apologize for what my imaginative mind thought of. She managed a smile and said, "Oh no, don't cry". There was compassion in her eyes and softness in her touch. She said, "Baby, my tears have nothing to do with you. It's my history. I just want better for you than the life I've had. Today is the day I'm releasing my anxiety and starting to forgive myself.

My eyes anxiously searched her face because I couldn't understand why she should say such ungodly words like "forgive myself". I asked Mommy what happened. She began crying more intensely. For a while she said nothing. The silence was difficult to cope with because I didn't know what to expect.

Finally, she said this happened when she was about 10 years old. Now my mind was relieved because I thought it was because I broke her glass.

Momma dried her face and began talking. Quietly, as if she was afraid someone would hear her. I noticed the fear on her face. Life has been strange and different for me since that day. Phases for changing seasons. My mommy Julia Smith said to me that as a child she took care of her sisters. While her mother and father worked in the field. On one particular day, nothing was unusual. Her mother Henrietta Smith began preparing her morning routine for work as usual. She put me in the chair, put the rope around my waist, tied it to the chair then put her baby sister in her lap. She then tied my baby sister to me, securing her tightly. This was nothing new. This was her daily duty to sit with her baby sister tied to her lap. Her mother would put her food and diaper where she can get them until she came back at 12 o'clock.

For dinner, before her mother left, she put an extra cup of water to drink where she could reach, making sure she could not get up. Off they went to work in the field- from 7 A.M. to 12 noon. It was cold and the fireplace was stacked with wood to last until noon when the whistle would blow (they called it Big Jim Blow). Then the families would return home for dinner. It was nothing unusual about that day. Momma said her sisters were playing as usual.

The baby tied to her waist was asleep. Lenora was playing in the corner of the room. She began making louder playful noises. Running and walking around in the room, suddenly she heard screaming. I tried to move to see what was happening. My movement was limited because I was tied to the chair. Momma said she tried to turn the chair over, but it too was propped to prevent movement. I couldn't do anything but turn my head. The cup of water Momma left had been wasted as Lenora knocked it over when she ran.

Momma said her clothing had been too close to the open fireplace. "Fire! Fire! Fire"! I screamed but no one heard. Momma and Daddy was in the distance doing field work.

I yelled to Lenora to come here. She continued to run, jumping up and down, calling me Sug. "Help me! Sug!

Help me!"

Living in the 18th -19th century early years, slavery ended yet in some areas men and women were used without knowledge that slavery was over. Later began crop-sharing, which was still limited with supervision. Working hard to sell crops just to pay off borrowed money. In debt, forever still slaves to the system.

What are we today? Slave to debt to pay off one debt to become the owner of a greater, more extensive agreement. Many times, overwhelmed, losing what little you have invested, hoping to acquire the greater gain.

Coping Strategy

I must deal with the events of yesterday.

I cannot run away; I must face the horror of yesterday. IF in the eye of circumstances this is the present. A strong black woman who failed to let life pass her by. The letter (I) in the word (IF) is that woman who refuse to be defeated. She is standing beside the bent letter f sometimes known as fear. This woman sees it as faith in God, not fate she grasp it with all her might, pulling it to her breast to lean upon that solid rock. The capital F has a bar across the middle and a bar at the top that represents Destiny with choice. Take it or leave it. The choice is yours. You can choose this F and continue to plummet in history for a review lesson.

Step into the maze and experience the choices that I chose to live. Whether it is past events that brought me to this point or is it just for curiosity spurred from my refusal to become a conventional Woman. Even at the least of my trials I must get credit for acknowledging my imperfection. If' will always exist in one form or another. What is done with the deceitful If when it appears, is the issue that need attention? The (ifs) must be investigated for closure. *I must arise to take my stand. I am that woman naked and not ashamed.*

Cycle Phase

I'm in the dark, I feel myself floating in a cylinder of despair, it's like a magnet drawing me toward thousands of tiny lights. Oops one of them have trapped.

Me.

I must force my self to break free. I cannot move forward, I'm attached. This speck of light won't let go. I'm moving faster, I feel myself sliding against a wall. I'm stuck in this big tunnel; I cannot get free. I feel water around me, I've never felt that before. I do not know what is happening. I'm beginning to feel like a big ball floating in a sack. I'm touching something, I can move them, its fingers. I'm rolling around in a sack. I feel myself kicking. I don't understand this emotion, why am I kicking. I'm in the dark its quiet in here except an occasionally a rumbling noise. I'm frighten in here. I cannot imagine where I am and why my feet keep kicking as if trying to break free. I feel pressure — someone is pulling my body. I do not want to go, I can hear voices, — You're almost there. Push, push I could hear voices again saying Push. I'm thinking I do not know how to push. What is push anyway, I'm in this dark tunnel I can feel metal clamps on my head. I can hear the voice scream push, push. Harder, I feel myself being pulled out. I'm sad, I begin to cry. I'm sad, I don't know if I'm going to like this place, it's too big. Voices all around me laughing, some were crying, look she has my eyes. All I wanted to do was cry and kick my feet.

This little baby girl will be a woman someday *naked and not ashamed.*

Feeling of Rejection

In the public eye she is adored and worshipped with external appearance to the beloved one. Instead, she lives.

In fear of being punished because someone spoke a compliment or admired her beauty. She cringes with fear because this may be mistaken as overt flirting. Fear set in as the smile upon his face become a smirk, as silent abuse begins. The solitude of her home becomes a prison known only to her close friends.

I live the life of servitude from sun up until sundown. This true story that was lived through a hellish existence. Not cherished or loved but another person to be the focal point to release hostile emotions upon. The pain felt was easily masked. The shamed I dare not tell who will believe. Therefore, to continues the masquerade of pretending to be happy became my lifestyle.

I sought comfort in knowing that God was not a sleeping giant. One crucial moment, I was found sitting on the step of my mother's house sobbing. Silently by my side my brother put his arms around my shoulders as the tears ran down my cheeks. He leaned over my shoulder whispered in my ear Sis you do not have to live like this. You should never be the object of person anger; you are my beautiful little sister. I'm your big brother and I do not like that behavior in a man. Furthermore, you are not a punching bag you are a woman. You may want him, but you surely do not need him."

I thanked him today for my mental support and guidance through those trouble years. As I look back at those days when I was so depressed because of the hat I chose to wear. Today I can truly say without a doubt, *I Am a Woman naked and not ashamed.*

Flash Back

When past events linger longer than a fleeting moment need to be settled. I remember kneeling at the altar to pray my heart was so heavy and unable to say a word, there was only weeping.

There were words in the dictionary to describe my feelings. My life was like a horror movie. I dare not tell who would believe. After a while I got up and went on my journey. Thinking back to that day God had heard my heart cry. Fifty years later, I visited that dark night of memories of the past. They are still bitter, but I can smile instead of trying to pull my hair out. I worked the night, and it was my night off, I retired to bed early just as I was dozing off to sleep my husband came in the room brushed my cheek with a rose and kissed my lips. Oh, I forgot to tell you the Veteran Club is having a meeting tonight, I won't be gone long. I doze off to sleep, when the telephone rang it was my supervisor. She blurted out, "Julia I need you to come to work tonight two nurses call in sick and with you off we are too short staffed I will give you tomorrow off with a long weekend you will have five days off together, I need you desperately tonight," she said, "all four labor room are full and both delivery rooms are in progress," I nodded my head saying "yes" and went back to sleep. Suddenly, I was awakened in a cold sweat my heart was beating fast I got up quite puzzled. The feeling went away, I had not gotten my uniform ready therefore I begin preparing for work being pregnant I moved about a little slower than usual. I called a cab for transportation.

I arrived at work. I reached for my assignment one of the nurses said don't give her that side of the hall its heavy she came in on her night let her have the lighter assignment. That did not go well they began to bicker among themselves.

It was settled I got the original assignment just as I begin to make my round to check my patients one of the nurses called me, was flush tears in her eyes she said Julia don't go in that room. I'm puzzled, I began to rationalize it's the open unit they wouldn't have contagious patient out here. I continue making rounds I knocked waited to be announced a voice said enter therefore I precede to enter the room ahead of the other nurse. As I walked past the first bed, I felt a wave of nauseous rush over me my knees began to tremble cold sweat engulf my body again I felt my heart beating fast, the same feeling I felt before leaving home. I leaned against the bed to steady myself. After a moment I focus my attention to my assignment opening my eyes the patient looked in my eyes her visitor had his body over her kissing her neck. For a moment I was frozen in time that's my husband. I was in a horror zone having to keep my sanity and to fight to maintain my dignity. I almost fell in the bed. The other nurse called my name Julia don't go there!

I did not know, but I knew I had to do something. The freshly filled pitcher of ice was at my right hand I felt my hand pushing the pitcher on the floor. The nurse that was accomplishing me tripped over her cart spilling ice on the floor. We left the unit the two of us took a sick day. Thinking about it now, I have mixed emotions.

Naked and not ashamed

Memories Linger

My heart is pounding as the tears flow from my eyes, as I read the divorce decree, I knew then I must stop digging in this chest of memories that housed madness and move forward.

If I linger longer in this maze with this mindset it will only reflect the conflicts of yesterday and hype the pain of regret. I might get stuck, and its possibilities of the "IF" will come true, or the possibilities will show that the truth I found prolonged my inner peace as I drank from the fountain of life. Thirst for inner peace. Still seeking the Inner Peace.

Divorce is worse than death There is closure in death. Death is final nothing can make it better nor worse it's over. Tears are natural, they cleanse the soul; you will always miss their presence. Divorce is the opposite when children are involved. There is that physical contact and the constant reminders of yesterday that ignite the fight or flight syndrome (you failed again). It is not the physical contact you seek it is the avoidance of friction and broken promises even though you are alienated. You find yourself encountering that person. He remains in your life but not of your life. It's just a generic fractured family.

I must hasten to catch up with "IF" and try to explain that I am not afraid to peek behind the curtain. I know now not to leaned on the IF' trying to forget the past. What If What If Naked and not ashamed to finally reveal the Perfect Black Pearl.

My Prayer

Here I am Lord bent and broken, I have made my life a mess, please take it.

And fit it in your master plan to use as desired for the glorify of your kingdom.

My Spirit is sad, my soul is perplexed, and my body is broken, only you can fix. Can you fix me, or will you fix me? I'm in a mess and I can not live like this.

Here is my heart Lord be merciful and change me.

Examine me from the outer most to the inner most.

Reveal my soul agenda hidden as it maybe, naked only to. You are the core of my being.

Set me free from this inner turmoil of yesterday that has held me hostage and have blighted the beauty of my essence.

Let me feel your presence as I draw nigh to that Tree, where You shed your blood for me.

Paving the way for all to see. You do not have to hide and feel the shame. The blood that Jesus shed gives that glorified covering for the soul.

The waves of humanity may come again and attempt to ignite feelings of shame.

Just remember:
Jesus gave his life for all to see, if you draw near to Him, you can be.

Naked and not ashamed

I forgot that my husband would be waiting and that he was very jealous and that his jealousy ran wild If I was a few minutes late. I was thirty minutes later than usual. After arriving home, I apologized he said that alright. I picked up the baby and the other children ran up the stairs laughing and playing ahead of me. Just before I arrived at the top stair, I felt a swift jerk on my hair. I felt the wind beneath my feet as I was falling backward down the long flight of stone stairs with my baby in my arms. I was shocked, I had to act quick our life was threatened. As I was falling my arms curled around my baby holding him snug well against my breast to keep him safe. I fell down that flight of stairs on the stone floor. I checked my baby he was laughing the fall amused him. I knew he was alright. I looked up my husband had his foot ready to kick me, I rolled over quickly to get out of his way. Oh, I felt like killing him, I pick up a clay pot with a flower in it that sat at the base of the stairs and aimed it at the back of his head. I was very angry, that fall could have killed us. Before I could hit him, I heard a loud voice "Don't if you hit him, you'll kill him." I put the pot down picked up the phone and called for help. Help arrived, I took my children to my mother's house, and there we remained for a season.

Naked and not ashamed

"Never Will I leave you, Never will I forsake you" (Hebrews 13:5)

We were both very young when we got married. He left college went into the Army. After his tour of duty was finished, we returned home to continue our education. We had already began our family. Our children did not announce themselves; they came and before long our family had grown. I continued in nursing school he continued in college... Life was great or so I thought, until one afternoon my doorbell rang, and I answered it. There stood a young lady smiling, she greeted me as if I was a long-lost friend. When I open the door two of my children rushed out. She replied, you have such beautiful children. Her eyes had an innocent look as she smiled. I'm your brother's girlfriend and I wanted to meet his nieces and nephews. As she talked, I felt sorry for her being deceived by a married man. As she was leaving, she asked me to tell him.

His classmate came by, and she will see him tonight when he comes over. It was all I could do to contain myself and to keep my composure. This was my first encounter of my mystery man. Of course, He denied it. She is just a troublemaker, he said. I was heavy with child which was due at any day. Therefore, I put it to rest often. My baby was born I returned to school. Continued life as usual until one afternoon, I asked him to watch the children because I wanted to go to the pharmacy. He agreed, I kissed him and stated I'll be right back. While walking to the pharmacy I meet one of my classmates who informed me that our friend Nancy was home from the hospital.

Immediately, I felt guilty because I did not visit her while she was in the hospital, therefore I agreed to visit her. She lived about one block from where I was going. When we arrived, she said to me, "I know you are busy and always in a hurry when you visit me". I do not blame you.

Reflection

I am awake my mind is fully alert the air is filled with fresh fragrances in the crisp morning air. Thoughts are racing through my mind. The perplexities that are encountered in the realm of child rearing make life a maze to endure. Single parenting in this society is a full-time job. Rearing children in an abusive environment is worse than being absent of male role model. A divided family foster fracture personalities in the children. The clamor an uncertainty in daily living that our children are exposed to take away from their sense of wellbeing.

Trying to juggle the multi tasks that life presented became overwhelming. Locked away in my world trying to make sense of this madness, all I could comprehend "you are alone", what will you do? I remember going to my room closing the door behind me, sat on my bed and sobbing. I cannot remember how long I sat there, somewhere between dusk and dawn I finally moved. I went into my bathroom began rumbling through the medicine cabinet. I was looking for something at that moment, I don't know what. The feeling of helplessness had marooned into a deep feeling of hopelessness. I no longer felt pain my body was numb. There on the top shelf was a bottle of turpentine, I reached for it, opened the bottle and put it in my mouth. As I was about to drink when I heard the children crying. Over their tears I heard my younger son say, "Oh Lord what are we going to do the Rock is crying". That got my attention because I had masked my hurt without showing emotions many times before this incident. Instantly I had a flash back of being slapped so hard I felt woozy, I did not shed a tear then because my children were present. Immediately I saw my life fleeing in front of me.

No one wins in suicide, all loss. How I have reduced my life to the brink of suicide. I dropped the bottle got in the shower fully dressed shoes and all. The cold water was the tranquility I needed shock me to reality.

The wet clothes were put in the trash. I put on my happy face walked calmly to kitchen to cook, my elder daughter had cooked dinner. She looked at me with a broad smile and announced that dinner was ready. Everyone took their place around the table. This was truly a Kodak moment. She served black eye peas and rice, the peas were snow white large as marbles, and hard as a rock. She proudly announced, "momma I poured the whole box of salt in." I could not hurt her feelings. Everyone was silent and quite relieved when someone suggested hotdogs and French fries, which I gladly prepared.

After having lived in an abusive marriage the idea of single parenting felt mighty good. The house became a home where the children could be children not trying to referee fights between mom and dad or put in the middle of who is right or wrong. Its over whelming to think about those trying years... Thoughts of the abuse I suffered have been a living nightmare. Even in my work arena there were conflicts beyond reason, and the thought of having to go home to a living nightmare was unspeakable, but I endured.

For a fleeing moment, I could have pulled my hair out. All that kept me from losing my mind was God. I found in Him a quiet place that I could know peace, and although I was trapped in a maze of past events that kept repeating itself. I was in Love, and at times I thought it would get better. Naked and not Ashamed.

Roll back the Curtain!

I am at the window looking through smoke lens glass the pain in my soul.

Reflecting the dark cloud of despair hovering over the atmosphere. The memories appear as a wall held together with threads of teardrops. The curtain hides the true essence of the moment. clouds appear and some disappear, slowly floating me on a pilgrimage of which, I fear. In my mind these clouds appear full of laughter mystic cruising on silver coils luring me to peep behind the horizon, holding a starling mystic in their movement. As if to say come away with me, as if searching for the weakness in my garment. I dare not peep behind the curtain, yet I find it tinseling at the moment. Maybe a storm? I do not know.

My heart is heavy. I'm tempted to peek. I hesitate yet the feeling of curiosity is overwhelming, it's telling me to go ahead.

Caught in a cluster of memories dark as night...

My body began to shiver as reflections become transparent clouds representing phases of my life.

Events buried in the storehouse of yesterday's trophies. The curtains are beginning to appear as vivid as the cloud above. I'm almost tempted to close the curtain.

I cannot, I need to free of yesterday's clutter in my soul. Surviving in society today is a task which present a dilemma difficult to comprehend. The ills women are confronted, it demeans the energy she brings to the union, instead of embracing her strengths and cherishing presence.

She serves her family graciously while receiving nothing in return, even not a kind word. Oh, what a life!

Sheer Determination

My survival is due to my determination not to live a defeated life. Therefore, I needed to know more about myself. The thought of reliving the past is unthinkable. I must come to grip with my presence and the essence of who I am, I need to understand my strengths and to define my weakness. Even though I knew better I chose the familiarity and lean toward the comfort zone, which is not a challenge nor is it compatible to my strength. Therefore, it's alright to picture ourselves in the role of a servant for Christ. Jesus Christ our Lord and Savior blessed humanity via of the cross a suffering Servant... He came, He went, and He is coming back again. He suffers in our stead bridging the gap between eternal life and for a life void of the Love of God, where hopelessness and helplessness abound in a world without Love... He did it all to give me freedom from the wages of sin.

Remembering that Jesus paid my sin debt on the cross is the reason I became serious about not living in an abusive marriage. I must maintain my mental sanity as well as my physical health for my family's sake as well as for my own self.

Even at my greatest temptation or my weakest moment my trials all seen trivial in view of Calvary. The price Christ paid for me to have peace. Now I can feel whole again, because the prince of peace lives within this broken heart of mine.

Sitting at my desk to write this Phase of my life.

Tears began flow just the thought of yesterday's madness surface in my mind. How could I let myself stay in that abusive relationship? To this day forty years later I'm still puzzled. Thoughts about the physical and mental abuse still haunt my waking moments of why and how I allowed myself to remain in that environment.

Two reasons: 1. He adored the children; 2. I was the object for his abuse.

How many families suffer when abuse is left to run on its course. I know now you do not mean for it to happen, but you are trapped in phase of low self-esteem call love. Unless the victim gets help it will end in a tragedy for all involve. The knock down drags out fights to suffer though that while your children watched Is truly bedlam You suffer but the children carry the scars of combat fatigue as a fractured family.

It's <u>all in the name of love.</u> Yesterday was so vivid it seems as though I'm still trapped in the past. I must focus on the present to maintain my sanity.

The Curtain is Opening

I'm lying on the floor I'm trying to think why am I down here?

What happening? Did I fall? I could not remember why I am on the floor therefore I lay these Moments later felt a pain around my neck I've been choked but why? I began to pull myself as I crawled over the floor to the sofa, my head was throbbing, I'm he sofa, my head throbbing, I'm trying to think what happened? Why was I on the floor? Finally, I was able to crawl to a sitting position on the sofa. It's all coming back to me; this is Saturday the day before Mother's Day. My husband brought a large bouquet of red roses which he picked from his mother's raised Garden. He stood before me smiling, "*I thought you would like these.*" I took the roses put them on the dining room table. We smiled at each other, even gave me a kiss. I remember him saying, "*I've got to run an errand I'LL be right back,*" then we will have dinner. My heart was overwhelmed with joy hasten to fix his favorite foods, I requested my mother's help, who lived a few houses down the street. She helped decorated the table then she went back home. I'm still trying to recall, did I fall? I cannot remember. While sitting on the sofa the doorbell rang, I straggled to answer the door. To my amazement a florist with a huge bouquet of red roses larger and twice the beauty of the first eagerly handed me the flowers as he walked away. He said, "*Happy Mother's Day.*"

I'm in a fog I do not know what has happened to me. I'm leaning against the sofa hearing footsteps on the porch the door opens slowly as he walked in. I did not send those roses to you bitch; I sent them to my woman. I went into shock;

I did not know it at that time. I was still in a fog from earlier. He was so consumed with anger I tried to scream, remembering the glass window was behind my head as he charges me with brute strength, he knocked my head through the glass window. The jiggered pieces of glass cut my throat out, warm trickles of blood were running down my neck.

I thought "I must be dreaming or having a bad nightmare," I must wake up soon. I'm afraid if this is a nightmare, I must wake up now. I know this cannot be real (my knight in shining armor would not hurt me) This cannot be real. How could he hurt me or what made him act like a wild man.

Here I am lying with my head in the window, broken glass all around me and blood running down my chest. I began to know fear. I did not know what to do my neck was bleeding I did not know how intense the cut was. I was frightened, I did not know how or what to do.

In my mind I just couldn't believe that he had done this vicious thing to me. This is real, truly I'm living it.

I remember thinking I cannot move I do not know how intense these injuries were. At that moment, I heard the door opening. I could hear voices, heard someone say, "bring me a basin of water." I felt my head being gently lifted out of the window. I could hear them say be careful, "the glass is in her neck, hold her still, break the glass under her head then let her down gently." Someone placed a white towel over my face gently washing off the blood.

Their hands were so gentle, and I opened my eyes to see who had come in to help me. My head felt heavy as my neighbor held me gently. She said, "It's not bad I'LL fix you up real good, the wounds will heal eventually no one will see any scars." She gave me instructions to wear a high neck blouse then no one will be the wiser. She said to me, *"Don't try to apologize for his sick behavior. He's gone now we've seen to that. He wanted to hurt you again."*

I'm really awake this is no nightmare, it's real. I had been knocked through the window with people looking on. They were there and helping clear the broken glass and had taken the children to safety. One lady told lie still your mother has the children. I'LL be back to check on you. She paused, I'm your neighbor I live next door. *"I saw the whole thing!"*

In the blackness of my soul all that was left of me was rejection. It was silent for a while even my mind was quiet, but I could hear the voice of my neighbor saying, *"you'll be alright for now." "You've got to make a change."* He does not love you; you are his possession he loves people to admire your beauty. Then he punishes you because people like your warmth. You love him but that kind of love is toxic can't you smell the fumes? Remember this is not the first time he abused you, have you forgotten the incident on the steps? She walked away shaking her head.

I went to my mother's house to heal.

Naked and not ashamed.

Transparent

I'm transparent in deeds and actions I'm willing to view each day with all its awareness as a mirror of the past which never to be repeated. This is the bridge to the other side of nowhere. If I continue to wear rose colored lens blocking out reality just to live in the moment. No where will become my reality. It is the hidden treasured moments that are exposed becomes someone else mirror image. It will make the difference and I can give it away without a second thought.

The fire in my eyes ignites the desire to mask the pain of the past. No one must know the hell of being provoked to fight. For some it is a passion, other's it is a nightmare. How to break the mirror image of a shattered woman would be putty in the hand a careless person whose self is the Master and inflict pain is their passion. The place to nowhere may lead to masking the strength within that makes you whole.

The choice you make will determine your destiny it will mirror your path or shatter your destination. It is my decision to become transparent the vast majority of abuse isn't of the children. Abuse crosses the boundaries of gender, race, creed and culture. Maybe my story will enlighten someone trapped in a cycle of circumstances that lead to despair, I pray my story will help.

Someone else to know freedom from their past just as I now have freedom to have my own identity.
The road back to wholeness is an uphill journey, it's long and difficult. I can't give up that's not a thought. I've climbed over too many hurdles to give up. I know I can make it.

Subject: Continue Forever Love

Family:

CARLOS R. ROBINSON
MICHAEL A.ROBINSON
STG. VELMA CEPHUS PHD
ZELDA THOMPSON RNC
JAMES T. ROBINSON
CHARLES X. ROBINSON
ERIC L.ROBINSON
SHARRON S. ROBINSON
VENETIA W. CARTER, M.A.
JULIUS R. WILCOX
CLEVELL B SEALS

Significant: Great Women:

MOTHER DAISY MOSLEY
MOTHER MARIE TUKES
ELDER BARBARA SMOOT
SANDA BROWN
GLORIA DELORIS BROWN
ELDER THEONITA DAWKINS
DOROTHY M.PETERSON
FRANCES MOSLEY
CLAUDIA JOHNSON
LULA GILLIAM
MABEL NEITHER
BARBARA JEREMY
RUTHLYN JASMINE
MOUNTAINSIDE SEVENTH-DAY ADVENTIST CHURCH
PASTOR OSCAR SHERROD

Printed in the USA
CPSIA information can be obtained
at www.ICGtesting.com
LVHW060422290624
784298LV00004B/39

9 781959 930624